A
WOMAN
UNASHAMED
and Other Poems

BOOKS BY *PAUL ENGLE*

American Song

Break the Heart's Anger

Corn

Worn Earth

Always the Land

West of Midnight

American Child

The Word of Love

Poems in Praise

Golden Child
(libretto for an opera
composed by Philip Bezanson)

An Old-Fashioned Christmas

EDITOR OF:

Midland

O. Henry Prize Stories

On Creative Writing

A
WOMAN
UNASHAMED
and Other Poems

PAUL ENGLE

Random House   New York

FIRST PRINTING

© *Copyright, 1962, 1964 and 1965, by Paul Engle*

All rights reserved under International and Pan-American Copyright Conventions. Published in New York by Random House, Inc., and simultaneously in Toronto, Canada, by Random House of Canada Limited.
Library of Congress Catalog Card Number: 65-11277
MANUFACTURED IN THE UNITED STATES OF AMERICA BY
The Haddon Craftsmen, Scranton, Pa.

DESIGN BY TERE LOPRETE

The following poems have appeared previously:

Verses from "Notes," "Variations on Love," and "Lament," in
a poem entitled "Variations"; a verse from "Party," in a poem
entitled "Shadow"; "Encounter" and "Lighting," in *Harper's
Bazaar;*

"The Ending," as "The Ending—Tokyo: A Woman Speaks,"
and "Ballet Rehearsal," in *The New Yorker;*

"The Word and the Poet," in the *Saturday Review;*

"Edmund Blunden on His Sixty-fifth Birthday," in *The
Texas Quarterly;*

"Letter about Love," in the *Ladies' Home Journal;*

"A Bar near Shibuya Station, Tokyo," "Taichung, Taiwan,
Republic of China," "Venus and the Lute Player," "Hercules
(Drawing a Bow)," and "Etruscan Vase in Form of a Cock,"
in *Poetry;*

"Blind Man," in *Focus-Midwest.*

To my lifelong friends and neighbors,
Owen and Leone Elliott, Marvin and Winifred Cone,
of Cedar Rapids, Iowa, who have also been
lifelong friends of the arts.

POEM AND PADDY FIELD

Paddy field, where the straight rice grows
Out of the water-loving land,
And poem where the straight line flows
Out of the word-caressing hand,
Need the same effort, row and line
Inch by inch: A human knack,
A vision of a green design,
Devotion, and a bending back.

Contents

(*x i i*)

I

A
WOMAN
UNASHAMED

(In Tokyo, 1963, a Japanese woman told me the story of her love for a man. I can still hear her sad and candid voice.)

) KITE

As a little girl, I admired boys
jerking the strings of their paper kites,
making them wriggle in the remote wind above me,
high in the bird-bright air.

Now, older, walking this garden on top of the hill,
I am above the kites boys fly
with curving strings, from the crooked streets below.

Now I am part of that sky.
Looking down, it seems as if the kites are really flying
    the boys,
as they run through the streets,
tied on the end of the pulling strings.

I have such lightness when you come.
Hold my hand, or I will blow
right off of this wind-reckless earth.

) FATHER-IN-LAW

A frog croaks in the garden pond outside.

Beyond the screen
where you have gone to welcome our guests,
I hear the fat voice of my father-in-law.

I think of you.

Yes, I will pretend
his voice is as pure as the cooing of pigeons.

) NOTES

Butterfly trembles when the wind blows.
You walk near me.

The dog barks at the loud moon.
When you come to me,
I speak softly, softly,
until we are silent together.

For two hundred years
this pine tree has been trained to grow sideways.
I have known you only one week,
but I bend as you walk toward me.

In the garden, you talk to me.
I do not want to
reply or shake my head.
Even my hands hear you.

Above the fish pond
the butterfly seems to listen
to the red azalea speaking.

The squirrel quarrels with the branches
through which it flies.

The sun quarrels
with the shadows of leaves over the grass.

When I touch the terrible pleasure of your hands,
my mind quarrels with the tangle
in my throat and breast.

) PARTY

Opening the door,
With one foot lifted, I stand,
Because your shadow is there on the floor.
I cannot set my foot down
For fear of treading your shadow under my heavy gown.

Can't I just stoop and caress it with my hand?

I look at trees
without knowing I see them.

But when you enter the room
I can feel
the eye alive in my head.

In the crowd of people at the party
I see you talking to them,
but your eyes are turned away,
running around the room,
touching faces, looking for me.

Surely, sometimes, it is the leaf
which makes the wind blow.

Why does it take so many people
to get each traveler started on his journey?

Why all that shouted advice from men and women
to a young boy whose back is straight with fright,
who clutches his cheap brief case desperately,
as if it held his life, not just a clean shirt?

What can I say as you leave this city and me?
Shall I urge you— Be good! How foolish,
like telling a fish, Don't get your feet wet,
or a butterfly, Look out for high places.

I give you no advice but my own name.
Your hands lift toward me and I drop it in them
like a rare fruit brought from a far country.

You simply speak my name. I close my eyes
as if the sunlight spoke, and not your mouth.

) GOOD-BYE

Like a dog lost in the streets of a strange city,
I walk around this familiar room where my life
lies scattered over the floor, clings to the curtains,
stares with haunted eyes
from the sea-deep mirror which remembers your face,
and trembles from the chair you sat in, talking:

"This is good-bye. I will not be back. Good-bye."

Shouldering the air as if it were in your way,
you left, remote in your long bones,
the man whose mouth had groaned on my shaking shoulder.
Your square back shouted round words back at me:
I feel safe now, no longer violated by love.

Bits of me wander in the garden where we walked,
lost in the leaves, shuddering under stones,
prowling the depth of the fish-delighting pond,
Wherever you looked, something of me is left.

Did you know that love could tear a woman apart
like a bomb exploding or a maniac's hands?
It is noon. The glare of light where you touched my fingers
shrieks in my eyes. I close them like desperate doors.

And when the sun has been knocked out of the sky,
should I run crying over the grass,
trying to pick up night with my weeping hands?

(8)

) LAMENT

You are gone ten months.
Even the small bones in my
Body are lonesome.

There were two flowers in the garden today:
Azalea crimson in the bold sun,
and a bride rice-flour pale
when her new husband stared at her.

At midnight we could hear the moon
barking at all of the dogs in the world.

None of the garden trees had tops.
Night had cut them.

Darkness dissolved the leaves and crept
into the tiny space between blades of grass.

We were so close, not even the night air
lay between us.

Now at high noon, in your absence, the sun
is a living wound in the sky bleeding light.

) ENCOUNTER

Finding you, unexpectedly, in that room,
Was more than a mere woman in love could stand:
As if on a summer day, in the dazzle of noon,
One snowflake fell on my astonished hand.

) LIGHTNING

Under the willow tree, in the stormy night,
we huddled together
(for protection, you said, and I smiled in the dark).
Our backs ran with water.
The rain was black.
Where our bodies touched, we were warm and dry.

Then a shock of lightning,
gone in an instant, but I looked at you
moving a little away from me, startled,
and I cried in rage,
Too much light. Too much light!

) WATER COLOR

The painter puts two thin lines
on one side of the page,
and one line on the other side.
Suddenly grass grows there!

Between them, a wavering line.
Water is moving!

Your two eyes look at me.
You lift one hand.

Suddenly my heart is growing toward you.
Suddenly I am moving toward you!

) THE COMING DARK

Like a suspicious duck
Circling a pond which may hold either food or death,
Slow night uneasily settles on the earth.

My hand hesitates above your unopened letter.

) LETTER

I wanted to pick the flower
gay in the sun,
its petals glowing with light,
but left it there in the garden,
too beautiful to put in my humble hair.

Your letter blooms on my table.
I do not open it, in fear
it will say you are not coming again,
and I will tear up the roots of my life and die,
or in fear it will say
merely that you are not coming until night,
and I, alone in the hard sunlight of noon,
will cry:
Why are you not here now in my arms?

) DO YOU HEAR ME?

In the schoolyard down the street
children are yelling to be thrown the ball.
They beg with open mouths like little birds.

You do not speak to me in this crowded room,
although my eyes beg you. Merely because
I am a woman, I must not scream out loud.

I howl like a dog inside.

Do you hear me?

) CROWD

That vase of iris,
Silent, blue as your eyes,
Shames these bawling voices.

) THE ENDING

Should I not be ashamed
to lie on this brocade-covered bed
making these terrible noises out of my mouth,
like a shot rabbit or a dog hit by a car?

I go on screaming. I am not ashamed,
for are we also not animals,
born in another's blood, dying in our own?

I have been this way since yesterday noon.
It was precisely noon.
After looking at your posed face looking
toward that other woman posing by the pond,
I could do nothing but look at my foolish watch,
steadily ticking as if time were important.

In that garden where trees and blades of grass
were put in a careful order, she was a wholly
artificial creature, trying to be
more fluid than water, more supple than fish.

The day disintegrated around my feet.
I stamped the pieces into the soft ground.

Looking up at the burning sun I opened
my eyes wide and silently cried, Blind me!

The unmoved sun merely
put a dark dazzle inside my head.

I looked again at my watch,
whose tick was a second pulse beat on my wrist,

as if I really had somewhere to go,
as if there were really any place I could go.

A distant bell struck twelve times, telling the world
my love had just drowned in the pond.

Sunlight and time dripped out of my eyes.
I saw you suddenly in your full nature,
the tenderly tended, artificial man,
bones brilliant as porcelain,
eyes blue enamel baked in your head,
your face a fan opened to prove
every line of the landscape painted there.

Now I weep, in a woman's way,
less for the loss of love
than for the revolting view of your weakness,
naked there in the sun,
the little boy, whining for one more kite.

I cry. I am not ashamed.

And yet this evening, at the hot window
I felt that the horrible sun had set
not in the sky but there on my consumed hands
still burning from their final touch of you.

II

THE
WORD
AND THE
POET

I

Verse is not written, it is bled
Out of the poet's abstract head.
Words drip the poem on the page
Out of his grief, delight and rage.

Words hold his life, as window glass
Holds sunlight it allows to pass.

The word becomes the poem where
His pencil's point becomes thin air.

The word, which only tries to sing
A lived-through act, becomes live thing,
As if a mirror, black with night,
Turned the astonished air to light.

II

Beethoven, absolute of tones,
Lost his inner ear's fine bones.
Michelangelo, whose bright
Eyes could shape the shapeless light,
Lost at last his accurate sight.

Baudelaire, whose words could teach
Song to the birds, lost power of speech.
Through nights loud with the drunkard's shrieks
Evil kissed him on both cheeks.
Pelican in his stinking nest
Bit bleeding poems from his live breast.

Rimbaud, hell-haunted, bitter boy,
Piled grief on grief and joy on joy,
Made Paris seven-layered Troy.
His demon could not keep apart
Monstrous life and marvelous art.

Bellowing on the Montauk beach
Whitman made art from artless speech,
Yet it is not the naked man's
Barbaric yawp on those brown sands
Endures, but words that are the hush
Of Lincoln dead, the grieving thrush.

III

Man is the metaphor of is.
Verse is the metaphor of his
Abandonment of self, live man
Transformed to poem's formal plan.
Through brain and gut and furious heart
The artist dies into his art.

IV

Poems are the arrogance of men
Who think their own
Gayness and gloom are worth enduring again
In the breathing shape of words: as with the blunt
Point of a burnt deer bone
Cavemen carved on the limestone wall
The bison's bellowing fall,
Living again the blood and howl of the hunt.

Poems rise up, although they bear
Sorrows and joys,
As if men breathed the sunlight, not plain air,
Filling these human sounds with a live flame:
As waking boys
On the first winter night
Watch their warm breath turn white,
Proud as if it spelled their glittering name.

Poets, like pigs snapped at by fields they root in,
Or even more,
Like hoot owls haunted by the trees they hoot in,
Return in their own verse to their own pain.
The poems that they bore
In blaze of day or dark of sleep
Are ways by which they keep
Their marvelous madness in a world gone sane.

III

EDMUND BLUNDEN
ON HIS
SIXTY-FIFTH
BIRTHDAY

(In devoted recollection of Oxford, 1933–1936)

) EDMUND BLUNDEN ON HIS
SIXTY-FIFTH BIRTHDAY

) I

Soldier, teacher, scholar, man,
White-flanneled cricketer who ran
Wicket to wicket with his bat:
Should any life be more than that?

Yes—the poet, whom we blame
For giving joy and grief a name,
For looking up at the bold sky
Whose sun burns through the living eye,
For looking down where song has shown
The cricket under his cool stone,
For adding to each simple word
The wing and warble of a bird,
For making silences so clear
And absolute that we can hear
Time screaming in the frightened ear.

He taught how friendship first began:
To be a friend, first be a man.
I learned all that a student can:
To be a poet, be a man.

) II

On Cumnor hill we walked. We went off swinging,
While I stooped to a bright stone in the field,
Then threw it toward him, being far behind.

A startled fieldfare rose, swearing in singing,
Circled, and seemed to mutter as it wheeled:
Please mind your business with a little mind.

) III

Walking one day on Headington hillside
His foot spoke to the grass and it replied.

Walking into a grove where sunlight made
A shadow on a shadow in the shade,
We heard far off a country church's chime.
For one bronze instant we were out of time,
And out of place, until a bird song fell.
The living bird was louder than the bell.

Walking back home in rain, he slipped and fell,
But smiled in pride, knowing he could tell

That earth forever, like a massive root,
Would always proudly bear his falling foot.

Behind the limestone walls of Merton, gray
Out of the earth, twice-grayed with fog and smoke,
I brought my essay to him—how Donne broke
Verse with live speech, as we in our own day.

Stone stairway like a purgatorial mount,
Twisting as a drunken street in London,
I climbed up to the room of Edmund Blunden:
Uneasy Iowan, not much account.

Eyes met me, burning through the morning mist,
Shy creature, burrowing the autumn gloom,
Who seemed to haunt, rather than hold, that room:
Warm hand that clenched into a wiry fist.

Short, slight, he seemed assaulted by a chair,
But as he waited, such a radiance beamed
From his intensity of face, it seemed
An animated star were rising there.

"Written your essay? Good. Then we won't read it.
Late yesterday I saw you playing cricket.
Now let's suppose these volumes are a wicket.
Just watch. Here's some advice. I'm sure you'll need it."

He piled up books and crouched behind, pretending,
A wicket-keeper waiting for the ball,
Tutor become the eager player, all
His attitude transfigured, body bending.

He showed me how to swing the bat, not round
Like baseball, but flat-surfaced; how to meet
A ball thrown stiff-arm just before the feet,
Twisting as it spun up from the green ground.

But then he leapt, and cried exultantly,
"Bowled!" Knocked Donne and Marvell down, so both
Hit Chaucer, who swore an Anglo-Norman oath.
"Back to the clubhouse just in time for tea!"

Then turned and took from the ritual fireplace
The smoking pot, the smoky tea inside.
Instantly he was glowing friend, shrewd guide,
His face a sun at which I warmed my face.

) **v**

We walked Port Meadow where the distant towers
Of Oxford shimmered like a chime of hours,
When the gold sun pushed out between gray showers.

At Wolvercote we turned and heard them there.
Eternity rushed by us with a glare.
We almost trembled in that trembling air.

Rain hissed on the horizon, drowned that flame.
We tried to walk, and stumbled as if lame.
Each called the other quickly by his name.

Amazed that we could see and hear again,
We saw each other living, and learned then
Another meaning for the mean word—Men.

Picts were early Englishmen
Who painted their faces blue,
But really there's no need for paint,
Weather alone will do.

One day I met him. Sun had scratched
The Oriel tower with gold.
He shook my hand. His hand was shaking
With that May morning cold.

In all that radiance of light
We stood, and shook with chill.
At Magdalen the choir boys
Were singing sweet and shrill.

"Last First-of-May at Prattle Wood
I head the larks in air,
But could not see them, high above
The gray mist rising there."

He smiled, and such a human warmth
Rose on that bitter day,
It was as if we two had met
On earth's first living day.

Now when the world's hot atoms warn
Another age of ice,
I keep one simple wish: let that
Encounter happen twice,

Let one more May-Day morning bring
Me again to meet
Edmund Blunden shivering
Along an Oxford street.

The guns went off, and he went off to fight,
Too frail, too brave, too gentle and too young,
Found terror had a steel taste on the tongue,
The honest sun was wicked—it brought light.
A blue-coat boy, he learned that the blue air
Could darken with the sniper's deadly eye.
A soldier's way of living was to die.
Yet took a cheerful view of his despair,

Respected each man's fear, but honored more
The conquest of it. Knew gun, shell, gas, knife.
Caught in the open by the rocket's soar,
He knew the ordeal of the frozen wait,
Found death a landscape where he searched his life,
And hated most of all the shout for hate.

Windrush winding out of western hills,
The Evenlode by Woodstock, Wychwood, Combe,
The Thame where it ran down to meet the Thames,
The Cherwell reticent beneath its willows:
These were the streams he left to walk along
The valleys of French streams, but only found
Ancre and Somme had grown most peasant-wise:
Blood would turn a mill as well as water.

Abingdon, Water Eaton, Noke,
Saw us pass with laugh and joke.
Shotover Hill and Pixey Mead
Watched him striding in the lead,
His hands like birds beating the air,
Declaiming Shelley and mad Clare.

By Wytham Park at Wytham Inn
We had our choice of tea or gin.

By Horsepath once, by Brasenose Wood,
We walked beyond Great Milton, stood
To praise that poet, one who would,
Bearing his life beneath blind skies,
Glare back at God with his blind eyes.

By Kidlington to Hampton Gay
We walked one glittering spring day.
Pointing, he said, "That forest could
Have been the slope of Thiepval Wood
Above the Somme. My men were there,
But vanished into empty air,
When the great guns destroyed that land.

Not one familiar foot or hand
Was found, only a reddish muck
To show the nature of their luck."

Such anguish crept across his face
It darkened sunlight. In that place
We felt, as it sneaked by, scared death
Pour on us both its stinking breath,
Death saddened by an ancient shame,
Having brought men such pain and flame.

The bloody weight of that attack
Still bore down on his narrow back,
But then he smiled. I saw that black
Memory lift like a barrage.
Hard ground, high hill, were a mirage,
Old war was his reality.
Softly he turned and said to me:

I "will be going over the ground again, until that
hour when agony's clawed face softens into the smiling-
ness of a young spring day."

Abruptly, like a shell exploding,
I knew the great truth I was holding:
While this man lives anywhere in the world,
It is always spring somewhere in the world.

Battle he knew by simply being battered:
"One scarcely seemed alive and touching earth."

Cruelty made him kind, for he had seen
Torment so dense that it had made a dark
Wood through which he walked with stumbling feet.

Mad for sleep, yet bold in fear, he made
"That great march of the British past Poperinghe
To that screened corner by the Ypres asylum,"
Up to the Front, and found with nerve and luck
What human nature did to decent nature,
How quickly clever man had learned to smash
The old distinction between man and mud.

Birds that were blasted, some of them still singing,
The nimble creatures roaming field and stream,
The cattle shattered and the trees beat down,
These he lamented, but what most appalled
Was all that savage human loss:

"Killed were my old company commanders
Penruddock and Northcote (after a great display
Of coolness and endurance in the German third line) —
Laughing French, quiet Hood, a hundred more."

) XI

He knew those men who walked through solid fire
To hang their bodies on the bloody wire,
Who, in their dreams, in the exploding night,
Endured the deaths they joked about by light.
He knew that soldier who, with shocking fright,
After the brutal shellburst, smelled the stench
of his own brother garbaged in the trench.
He knew how soldiers, moving up, had sung,
How they had felt their fate was to be young,
How history was a rope from which they hung.

He knew (and ruddier officers turned pale)
"The slow amputation of Passchendaele."

And yet in love and courage that youth ran
Through the great wound of the world, soldier and man.

) XII

Some glowed like him in that dread darkness. When
Hurt England needed, more than moon or sun,
And more than starlight—*men*—those boys were men.
They fought and suffered. Thus the job was done.

) XIII

Deep in the dugout, under steel and mud,
He waited, and endured the monstrous shelling.
Down in that darkness, with the wounded yelling,
One candle shook and burned. It dripped live blood.

) XIV

He always kept an earned and honest hope,
Like a hanged man's expert knowledge of rope,
For those were men he loved, in terrible ways
No man loved woman—for the deadly days
They shared at Ypres, when an inch of space
Meant life or death—not mine, or his, but our.
Now still he waits that visionary hour,

"when it shall be the simplest thing to take
in your hands and hands of companions like E.W.T.,
and W.J.C., and A.G.V., in whose recaptured gentleness
no sign of death's astonishment or time's
separation shall be imaginable."

) **x v**

Now on this twenty-five-years-gone day, I lean to pick up his letter, as you bend in a blind room toward a switch on the wall, knowing that from the lift of your fingers sudden light will flow.

His letter, a light bulb radiant in the dark, illuminates that old reality, how he swung through his life with a squirrel's nervous nimbleness, quick in the sun, bright in the shade, trembling through trees.

All the world's waters might snarl at all flinching coasts, but in the human house of his presence I felt safe.

A quarter of a century since last I saw him; now his letter whispers on the table. It lies there in that sturdy gentleness with which he held cricket bat, gun, devoted hand, giving me once again a vision of his life: Playing field, battlefield, the broad meadows of books, all places of controlled violence and risk. Over these he moved, leading courage by one hand, decency by the other, a quiet proof of what the mortal race of men means when it produces a really good example.

Unread, untouched, the letter is a window through which I look, seeing beyond it his lively face, his agile hands gesturing, his feet walking the fieldfare-haunted fields.

The letter lies, an island in the dark sea of my desk, telling me that he was my island within the loved, shared island of England.

IV

LOVE

Your hand is home. Whether in light or dark
Like friendly dogs your fingers leap and bark.
The sun comes from the east, wind from the south.
I come from silence to your talking mouth.
I come to search with you over the wild
Landscape of love, and not as a lost child,
Frantic for any touching, warm and human,
But as a man, praising you as a woman.

We talk, and that is useless as to sing.
Our slick words mock this marvelous, plain thing:
A man gives so that he may ask to live.
A woman's way of asking is to give.

Live stars need darkness to reveal their light,
But love, that is our doom and our delight,
Needs neither day nor dark, but only being
Together, in one presence, closer than seeing.

For love, like weather, simply happens. No
Will, no thought—feeling's full overflow.
For love, all grace and lightness, needs no light.
Dear dark, come down. Our hands will be our sight.

Love saddens, too, with its ecstatic nerve,
By being more than men and women deserve.

I call you, in my lucky tongue's elation,
Not just a name, more like an incantation
By some old savage making the magic sound
Which calls his god to consecrate that ground,
Which makes vile devils scream and disappear,
Which draws the fangs from snakes, and frightens fear.

And I have heard your soft voice speak my name—
How small a sound to burn the ear like flame.

These words for you—love me as each one flies
Off of the page to touch your looking eyes.

) YOU

You are no slick siren in Hollywood,
Flourishing to the camera her bold face,
Nor the tape-measured blonde, having more grace
Than one bare woman, merely mortal, should.

You are the natural person without fame
Whose loveliness they cannot mechanize.
Life is your meaning. Love is how you live.
You are all feminine, and when you give
Yourself to the full shock of love, your eyes
Grow beautiful beyond measure or name.

) LUCKY ROOM

When you are here, I taste you like fresh bread.
Your presense gives a point to the vague air.
I turn and touch the turning of your head.
Your body strokes the fortunate, bold chair.
But when you go, then you are all around me.
I breathe you in the window's darkened blur.
Like your own arms the leaning walls surround me.
Rug turns voluptuous as a beast's fur.

The room's mouth cries: she loved you in this place.
The radiator hisses: I too warmed her.
The door brags: I'm the one who bravely shoved her
Into your arms. Mirror: I held her face.
Newspaper rustles proudly: I informed her.
The lamp: I sparkled on her when you loved her.

V

POEMS LIVED IN ASIA

) IN A BAR NEAR SHIBUYA STATION, TOKYO

The Japanese next to me at the bar
bites at his sake with big irregular teeth.
Behind the heavy glasses (which he wears
like an elegant suit of clothes) his eyes
are yellow as the warm wine he is drinking.

He turns like a door opening and says
with an aggressive softness, "USA?"

I nod, waiting to see the color of his mind.

"I was wounded at Okinawa."
The words drop reluctantly from his mouth
like drops of wine from the bottom of the bottle.

I set my weight on the soles of my feet
and keep a careful eye on his hands.
He pulls up his sleeve. The scar cries out
along his arm like an exclamation mark.
What words do you speak to an accusing wound?
He looks at the scar as a man looks at a bug
crawling his skin, with interest and loathing,
wishing that it would simply go away.

"I'm sorry," I say. The words in their silly weakness
vibrate in the vivid lamplight of the bar
before they fall to the floor with a shamed rustle.

He clenches and unclenches his fist. The scar ripples.

I lift my hands. I am ready, like a new kid
uneasy on a school ground the first day.

"American doctor fix my arm good," he says.
And then his face collapses into a smile.
"He not fix good, I not pick up sake now."

He lifts the blue-glazed, lovely curving cup
and gestures gently toward me. Shyly his eyes
move over mine like a friendly hand. We drink.

He puts the cup down carefully on the bar
with a brave lightness, as if it were a bomb
waiting to go off and blast his hand.

His face goes back to being merely a face.

Outside, Tokyo growls like a hunting tiger.

) TOURIST

I am an American tourist in my room writing letters.
Outside the air of Calcutta trembles in the terrible heat.
Air conditioning gently wraps me in cool air.
I call room service and the cold drinks
fly in like tame birds on my bearer's hand.

The Wisdom of the East, I decide, drinking,
would be wiser if it used more American devices
to give the body ease, thus freeing the mind
for meditation on eternity.

I sit there writing careful English,
wanting to make the deliberate phrases prove
that I really am here in an Asian country,
a jet-propelled Marco Polo,
my blood stream brave with shots and antibodies.

Outside the window, screams.
They go on and on, each an echo of the other,
in a dark, small, desperate voice.

I am outraged by that rage.

Who can write words, hearing that wordless noise?
Did I fly over oceans and mountains
to sit here and yell at that yelling?

I rush out to the street
wearing indignation and a dark businessman's suit.

Sound stops.

A thin and hungry woman has just given
her brown breast to a hungry child.
Nothing of her has fulness but that breast.

In this heat, even my eyes sweat!

I wrap my shame in a smile like spit in a Kleenex.

Near the American Embassy, on a low wall,
Two homesick ladies stare at the flapping flag.
"Mabel," the blonde says, "I don't want to nag,
But if I stay here, I'll just sit and bawl."

"Florence, I know, I know, I feel the same way."
(One was round as the world, and one was skinny.
One voice was soft as curd, one hard as a whinny.)
"I'll take a photo. We'll remember this day."

All over Asia cameras click with joy
At landscape, shrine, or temple wall carved high.
Two aging women take merely a flag in the sky,
But what they see is Oregon, Maine, Illinois.

) TAJ MAHAL, *Agra, India*

The Taj Mahal with its massive marble lightness
floats above the river valley, the most
beautiful building raised by a man to a woman,
nor was it built out of romantic folly
by an ignorant youth idealizing a lady.

Shah Jehan, absolute Emperor, had it made
in that pure femine form, bent like a breast,
to honor Mumtaz Mahal, simply a wife,
in the early seventeenth century when women
were things to be collected like tigers and jewels.
What a woman she must have been in such a time
to be given such grateful devotion after her death.
For twenty-two years he built it, in her praise.

She had borne him many children, surely he knew her
as well as a man could know a wife. Surely they quarreled
out of love, and were reconciled out of love,
made private family jokes, smiled at each other
riding on top of the rocking elephants,
giving a human touch to that royal pomp.

Inside the high and haunting tomb I marvel
at the colored flowers carved from pure gems and set
in the fiercely white stone, their long stems curving
lively and lovely as a woman's hair.

The guide calls, "*Allah ho akbar*," Allah is great.
The double dome reverberates, down to a whisper,
like the architect's echoing voice, proud of his work.

All day the dead wife hears God praised, and hears
footsteps of shoeless tourists rustle the floor.
With her fragile woman's bones she bears the weight
of all that old immensity of marble.
I leave cool darkness for the burning day
where the Indian sunlight bounces back from the stone
in a white echo.

A little girl
waits for her parents to climb the stairs. I smile.
She turns away, a disciplined, decent child,
huddled inside her orange-colored sari.
Then she peers shyly up, her face centuries old
with a woman's way of looking at a man,
shrewd, affectionate, timid, all in one glance.
Softly she speaks her two little words of English,

"Good noon," in a voice that is scared and poised together.

Then, with a hand before her mouth, amazed,
but also pleased, at such a brazen boldness,
she says again, more gently now, "Good noon,"
and flees into the Taj with a flutter of cloth.

The far sun wavers hotly at high noon;
its light rays shimmer from the reflecting pool.
My own eyes waver in the wonder of that child.

You taught me, little girl, about that Empress, why
an Emperor built her a tomb, over those years,
in desperate devotion.
Surely among women she was most womanly,
the sort who can move a man by more than beauty
so that, gone, she makes his unfulfilled hands
feel they can touch her again
yearning toward this eternity of stone.

You blessed that building, child,
with your small, feminine presence.

You will never have, living, the robes of Mumtaz Mahal,
you will never have, dead, so echoing a tomb,
but already you know more English than she did.
Already, finding the right and furious moment,
you have instructed and amused a man.

You will never live in a castle, ruling a country,
but in your time, like Mumtaz Mahal, you will be
that greatest wonder of our human world
before which tombs dissolve like sudden tears:
a wise and loving woman, alive. Alive!

) CHINESE GIRL, QUEEN'S ROAD CENTRAL, HONG KONG

I watched the girl on the corner wait.
Her skirt was tight. Her legs were straight.

Her skirt was split above the knee
(Vision, not leg, is what I see).

The features of her sunlit face
Gave the sunlight a living grace.

Fine neck not only kept head high,
But held up, too, admiring sky.

She stood with that instinctive ease
Of women knowing men will please.

One hand, lifted to pat a hair,
Caressed the touch-delighted air.

Then suddenly I saw her lean
Forward, and knew what that would mean:

A man, approaching on the walk.
He came up close. They did not talk.

They did not touch, but merely stood
In passionate, pure gratitude

That each saw each with loving sight.
Their noon became a love of light

Where eye caressed the other's eye
In silence that was like a cry.

They simply looked, but my eyes heard
Between them, their unspoken word.

) TAICHUNG, TAIWAN, REPUBLIC OF CHINA

In the soft and feminine valley the rain falls softly.

I feel it on my forehead, warm from the train,
like a hand saying, Cool. I will make you cool.

I slip and fall on the rain-wet stones.

The book I am holding flies out of my hand,
and stops in front of a thin young woman walking.

As I get to my feet, she bends down, taking the book,
bending and lifting in one long, graceful gesture,
her body curved as if all of it were an arm.

When she stoops, I see the baby on her back.

The child looks at me with calm, black eyes,
swaying a little as its mother moves.

Surprised at her act, the woman takes one step back,
her face uncertain and fearful, holding the book
as if it might explode.

She flinches at seeing the man before her is foreign,
at finding the book is a language she cannot read.

The rain falls shyly between us on that public street.
I walk up to her, holding out my hand.
She lifts the book toward me in a marvelous,
easy motion, as if she were giving my life
back to me, or light to the cloudy earth,
or her breast to the child, which peers at me under
her arm with a dark reassurance.

Her hand touches mine with brown warmth.
In that moment, the book has no weight.

Watching me watch her face, abruptly she smiles,
but startled again at her daring, she turns away,
graceful as water flowing, and walks down the street,
the baby bouncing happily on her back.

I stand in amazement, glad to have fallen there
on a Chinese street, mud like a blessing on my knees,
letting the rain fall over my head and hands,
onto the book, which suddenly seems absurd,
letting it fall on my mouth, which had not spoken,
and into the grateful marrow of my bones.

There, in Taiwan, even the rain is a woman.

) NISHIHONGANJI TEMPLE, KYOTO, JAPAN

The temple tower vibrates with the struck gong.
Outside the gate two boys play at ping-pong,
Their table simple boards, a stick across.
They yell like western kids at win or loss.
The god's great bell makes the bronze air ring.
The white ball of the boys goes, Ping, Ping.
When that bell booms, the sunlight seems to shiver,
The weightless ball, in mid-air, seems to quiver.
Will men forever hear that bell's singsong,
And, lucky, hear that hollow ball's ping-pong?

Near the great brass cannon where Kipling played as a boy,
A huddle of cloth hesitates at the curb,
Five feet, two inches of cotton caught by the wind,
Swaying in shyness back from the traffic's threat,
The tiny, darting cars, the jangling bikes,
The squeaking bullock carts bulling their slow
Progress down the street as if they pulled
With wrinkled necks and brutal shoulders, the whole
Reluctant world, and not a load of wood.

Around it are people walking, but what keeps
That gray-white softness erect in the soft air?
A car darts darkly by. The cloth shudders.
Gently the bundle takes one more step back:
No living shape, no person and no name.

Then suddenly a child shoots laughing out
Into the reckless road. Brakes snarl. Horns bark.

The huddle of cloth explodes into hands and feet,
Inside, a body trembles into life,
Darting after the child, down from the curb,
Snatching the boy with swinging arms. She holds him

Hard to her breast in that old mothering gesture
Ancient as childbirth and the human race.
She puts the boy down with a bitter word,
Collapses again into the cloth's limpness,
Once more a huddle of anonymous white.

Yet now the cotton trembles like a skin.
The hood (called burkha), worn by women in purdah,
For whom it is shame to show the world their face,
Falls again over head and neck, but now
Inside the woven window of the hood
A rapid breath flutters the threads with life,
And deep within, dazzling the burkha's dark,
A pair of burning eyes, a woman's eyes.

) KYOTO

Water and rock are planted as if grass,
The air cut into views like window glass.

From the dark depth of goldfish-flaunting ponds
Temples are mirrored upward through fern fronds.

Here silence, too, is given form and size,
And is astonished by the gay bird cries.

Perfect in pond, even reflected sky
Seems drawn there by a clever hand and eye.

Here fish, gray, spotted, gold, with languid eyes,
Leap from that formal water at quick flies.

Alone, in this place carved as by a knife,
Fish are the one exuberance of life.

Here human nature, nature itself deceives:
Did men rub green into those glossy leaves,

Pour perfume in that crimson peony,
Teach butterflies what wings were meant to be?

Leaving Kyoto, where railroad tracks are curled
By temples, I am back in the real world,

Where all is noise and power, the useful thing,
Where only iron wheels on iron rails sing.

Then suddenly, I lose the world of facts:
Between a small house and the railroad tracks

People (dark strangers I will never see)
Have built a tiny pond, and lovingly

Curved its crude sides, colored them green with moss,
And laid a crooked stone one foot across.

Rain gave it the gray color of wet ground.
Its careful shape reëchoes like sung sound,

One little corner of this little land,
Made perfect by a man's imperfect hand.

To know one artificial fact is my one wish:
Did that small, artificial pond have one live fish?

) BOMBAY, INDIA

Outside my hotel, in the crazy traffic stir,
The beggar women shuffle and wait. They greet
My foreign face with a cry of, Silver, sir?
The silver bells are ringing on their feet.

) HONG KONG

Firecrackers crackle, opening a new store.
A young man watching, eagerly waits for more.
The young girl, watching him, crackles with love.
Her head looks shyly down. As if from above,
He gives her a quick smile, looks back to the road,
Waiting to see quick smoke and noise arise.
Abruptly in her black and grateful eyes
The red firecrackers of her heart explode.

Rain falls on me, and on
The irrigation ditch.
The soil beneath my feet
Is fertilized and rich.

No taller than a stake
For tying beans up high,
A poor old lady comes.
I cannot see her eye

Because her back and neck
Are twisted half around,
All of her body stares
At the rain-reflecting ground.

I watch her walking out,
Shouldering a hoe,
To fields made in her size,
Tiny row on row.

Her spine curves like a C,
But does it therefore beg
For pity and despair
Like Lautrec's crooked leg?

No! For the food she grows
That Tokyo may eat,
Comes from determination
Perfect and complete.

Carrot long as her arm,
The rooted radish, bean,
Gave her that sturdy stoop
And turned her fingers green.

Not she, but I, need pity,
For thinking she deserved it.
No illness bent that back.
Her healthy labor curved it.

Her bowed spine bows to me.
A smile blooms on her face.
With graceless dignity
She gives my day a grace.

) YAKUSHIJI TEMPLE, NARA, JAPAN

"Ethel, if I walk one more step, I'll faint.
If you're in a hurry, go on. I'll sit here alone,
Maybe become the statue of a saint.
Already my feet are turning into stone.

I'm up to my eyes in Buddhist temples and shrines.
I've seen my last god painted in a cave.
I'm through gawking at gardens with stunted pines.
The next flower arrangement I need will be on my grave."

Her voice whines on. It has the edge of a saw.
Why don'tcha stay home, I think, with your family,
And let them have the bitter joy of your jaw?
I take another, harder look, and see

Under the ugly dress that she is wearing
The thick blue veins are swollen with child-bearing.

A blur of brown, large as a bullock cart,
Comes down the road in the brilliance of afternoon.
It turns with the turning road, crawling along
Like a solemn animal fulfilling its life,
Going to food or water or a mate.

Through all that landscape, under a rage of sun,
Only that figure moves, and without sound.
The daylight trembles beneath the sun's dazzle.
The green fields flinch and shudder in that heat.

Surely inside the brown and shaggy fur
Blood flows, heart beats, eyes stare, teeth wait to bite.

Surely it has been moving down that road
Two thousand years, in that determined way
Nothing can stop, or frighten, or slow down.

And now I stand in this glittering pause of time,
At the edge of a narrow road in a wide country,
Watching the thing approach.
                              Then suddenly
It turns into a load of useful hay,

Piled high, yet dragging on the ground. Beneath,
The long and delicate toes of a woman's feet
Walk that road, as old sun crosses the sky,

Remorseless and unstopping.
                    One slender arm
Curves upward, steadying the great load,
A lovely bend of bone under brown flesh,
The whole load balanced on a head rising
Gently and strongly from a sturdy neck.

The breasts beneath the crimson sari bulge.

Surely that face needed two thousand years
To learn such poise of patience.
                    Now the eyes
Flash at me one quick glance, then turn away,
Not in self-pity, not in human fright,
Nor any shame, but with the easy calm
Of a shy creature fulfilling its own life,
Walking to food or water or a mate.

) OUTSIDE TAIPEI, TAIWAN, REPUBLIC OF CHINA

At Lahore the language is Urdu, liquid and soft,
At Delhi they speak the harder Hindi, at Bombay,
Marathi, with a rolling of the head,
In the brutal heat of Calcutta, Bengali, speech
Of Tagore, that saint of sound.
       In all this talk
I do not understand one uttered word.

Now in this place, called by the early sailors
Ilha Formosa, meaning Beautiful Island,
They speak Chinese, and here I am ashamed
Not even to know what the little children say.
Surely the words in their rhythmical tones must mean—
Funny, rice cake, or the gay terms of a game—
But I am an ignorant man; to me they are noises.

Yet only men cut themselves off with words.
The language of animals here is the same I know.

Yesterday in a farming village, hens
Bragged of their eggs as if each were a bold
New World in space.

                                    Dogs on a distant street
Abruptly barked, and the dog in a nearby door
Muttered in his mutt's throat to prove his menace.
Under a thatched roof a pompous pig
Grunted an ecstasy of mud and swill
(Heard in an Iowa childhood, a fat sound).

From a green field cow mooed, its voice the white
Color of milk.

                                    I am humiliated
To understand the talk of animals
But not the human speech of women and men.

Then down the street, with a sound I recognize,
A figure runs, with a step I recognize,
A crying girl, lifting a hurt hand.

Her cry, her eyes, radiant with tears, I know.
My daughters taught me these.

                                    I am ashamed
At my delight in her despair, at finding
That feminine, that old, familiar sound,
Making me feel at home on a foreign street;
The absolute, child language of her pain.

) **PARK STREET,**
CALCUTTA, INDIA

Pausing against a building, out of the sun,
Weary of walking, driven, in that heat, dizzy,
I read cool words: This stone was laid by Lizzy,
The Wife of George, in Nineteen Hundred One.

I think of her, foreign (homesick?), standing alone
To bless that place, before she left in her carriage,
And ask: Did she and George have a good marriage,
Brilliant as sunlight, durable as stone?

Perhaps no beauty, still, she was his wife.
George wanted her plain name on his building. Grateful
To learn his love, I walk into that hateful
Sunlight, refreshed by Lizzie and her life.

) ANCIENT LADY, TOKYO

As if it were a loaded peddler's pack
She wears the embroidered obi on her back.

Like a stunted pine distorted out of art,
She bends around the tough root of her heart.

No human scene is absent from her face,
Crowded with crooked lines like an old vase.

She utters life, as wind howls in a word,
As blowing air is visible in a bird:
Nothing she has not seen, felt, touched, done, heard.

Her back is bent, as if upon it lie
The heavy sun and moon, the star-crammed sky.

Her eyes, having seen too much, look at the ground,
She stumbles, not convinced the earth is round.
Her world is only what her feet have found.

Like pain through an arm, she trudges down that street,
Defiant of the darkness at her feet.

By being merely a life-battered woman
She turns a hard street feminine and human.

More than it seems one ancient lady might,
She huddles down that road in a halo of light,
A live and colored lantern for my night.

) AN OLD SCROLL PAINTING, KAMAKURA, JAPAN

Massed mountains overwhelm the scroll with gloom;
Their shadows seem to reach across the room.

Clouds push the sky aside, while far below
Tall trees instruct the four winds how to blow.

Each thing here is inhuman, massive, free,
Save where a tiny house, under a tree,

With crooked, hand-carved wall and roof, is leaning.
It gives the cloud and mountain form and meaning.

VI

POEMS ON ART

) SELF-PORTRAIT

The paint explodes into a face.
The eyes accuse the painter— Can you hear?
And are you mad? This hat
Screams on my head in fear.
Is this a place
Called Arles? And am I in it? What was that,
A knife or brush? Equally to be feared.
The pigment prickles in my beard.
Turn the face a little flat
To show my one good ear.

(Vincent van Gogh, 1853-1890)

) LADY AT MUSEUM

She looks. The painting sees her from its place.
Her head leans toward that beauty and she sighs.
The colors shimmer in her colored eyes.
The painting paints itself upon her face.

) THE LETTER

She sits, the letter hovers on her hand.

Her dress, like her arm, is young and feminine.
She gentles the garden air that she breathes in.
Silence so dominates that it subdues
Even the glowing pigments in the paint.

The ribbon in her hair is a red flutter.

Her head is bent, her eyes bend toward the letter,
But do not read it, merely see the whole
Page in its presence, gleaming from his hand.

Is there dark anguish in that page's whiteness?

The letter perches. Will it fly away?

(*Jean Baptiste Camille Corot, 1796-1875*)

) VARIATIONS ON THE
GUGGENHEIM MUSEUM

A rattlesnake, ready and coiled to strike
If the Metropolitan lifts its massive foot.

The paintings cling along the walls like scales.

Piet Mondrian measures out sunlit space
And cuts it into squares as neat
As a Dutch housewife chopping meat,
Bending above it her scrubbed, orderly face.

A painting of a hole holding its head.

Kandinsky coruscates, the canvas quivers.
Reality distorts the artist's hand.

Although this place, in part, surely is his own,
The builder's name alone
Is lettered shyly in gray stone
Right of the door.
But next to it an emblem, like a roar:
FRANK LLOYD WRIGHT, yelled out in red, a bloodshot
eye,

Inflamed, still threatening, accusing—I
Do not die.

An untouched canvas, empty as closed eyes:
The brush moves and a blaze of blue flares up,
The canvas burns into its separate fields.
One corner snarls and slashes at another.
The quick line lunges and the painting lives.

Imagination is a hand that sees.

) ENGLISHMAN AT THE MOULIN ROUGE

The horse-faced dandy whinnies at the girls.

(Henri de Toulouse-Lautrec 1864-1901)

) FOUNTAIN — THE PLAZA

Dressed in its feathers, decent bird,
The pigeon flutters on the nude.
And yet the girl in her green skin
Is modest, the clothed bird is rude.

Her shoulders pour the moving air.
Her back curves down, pure and precise.
The pigeon stretches out its wing
And pecks with nimble beak for lice.

Always the jets of water flow.
Always the city pigeon rests.
Always this naked girl is good.
The sunlight glows on her bronze breasts.

Far in the background a blue mountain waits
To echo back the song.
The note-necked swan, while it reverberates,
Paddles the tune along.

The player is a young man richly dressed.
His hand is never mute,
But quick in motion as if it caressed
Both lady and the lute.

Nude as the sunlit air the lady rests.
She does not listen with her dainty ear,
But trembles at the love song as her breasts
Turn pink to hear.

She does not rise up at his voice's fall,
But takes that music in,
By pointed leg and searching hand, with all
Her naked skin.

Out of that scene, far off, her hot eyes fall,
Hoping they will take in
The nearing lover, whom she can give all
Her naked skin.

(*Tiziano Vecellio Titian, 1477-1576*)

) FLEMISH INTERIOR

These floors were painted with a cake of soap.

) BURGOMASTER JOHN VAN DUREN

The grease of gold has oiled these cheeks
Protected by a plump, black hat.
Below white collar, belly peeks
And rumbles proudly—fat, fat, fat.

(*Gerard Terborch, 1617-1681*)

) HERCULES

(Drawing a bow)

The power in this sculpture of a man—
Archer and athlete, godlike in head and groin,
Whole body bending to the bow's bent span—
Is not in shoulders or the muscled loin,
Nor in the bulging bicep, the taut gut,
But in the eye looking at empty air,
Amazed it will never find the delicate
Feathered arrow that is no longer there.

) STATUE OF A GENERAL

(At The Plaza, Fifth Avenue and Fifty-ninth Street)

Because in many battles he had bled,
Because of the lurid soldiers he had led,
The resting pigeon decorates his head
With a pinch of praise, color of bullet lead.

Behind, the building stands, a bastard palace.
On its stone wall, in jealousy and malice,
A boy writes (in a heart) —Eddie loves Alice.

Because earth turns in its astonished flight,
The sun exploding out of nervous night
Each day will decorate our world with light.

Because man's mind is noble, nimble, great,
The triggered bomb of earth with human weight
Floats toward ecstatic glory or dark fate.

And if bird, boy, green field, explode in sky,
Their bitter glare will decorate the sky
With a pinch of light, invisible to the eye
(If, in that savage space, there is an eye).

) PORTRAIT OF A WOMAN

Her dress is wine, her fingers drink their rings.
Her jewelry is noisy: stone that sings.
Her final pride, strutting on her lap,
A dog, mouth grinning with a tiny snap.
Over its head, her hand is lifted up.
The hand is bigger, plumper than the pup.

(*Paolo Veronese, 1528-1588*)

) BALLET REHEARSAL

Where the hand flutters and the brief skirt whirls,
The stiff-dressed man directs the supple girls.
Their lightness makes the air seem solid, where
Against the wall a man sits with a glare,
Heavy of belly, heavy in leg and eye.
Birdlike before him the deft dancers fly,
Floating above the floor, before they land
In the bold branches of his hairy hand.

(*Hilaire Germain Edgar Degas, 1834-1917*)

These are no fields a farmer's eye has seen.
Here is the growing energy of green.

That is no simple sky. Here is the loud
Clatter of wind lost in a cry of cloud.

This grain does not bend down as the winds pass.
Here winds are blown far onward by the grass.

And that uneasy sky is troubled too:
Should it turn pure earth-green or pure sky-blue?

What brought intensity to this plain farm?
That tension trembled in Van Gogh's thin arm,

When he did nothing for a week but paint
And sleep and paint and eat and paint and paint.

That bold, vibrating light was first refined
Out of his bitter radiance of mind,

His crazy fears, the horrors of his life,
Before he slashed it here with brush and knife.

(*Vincent van Gogh, 1853-1890*)

) ETRUSCAN VASE IN FORM OF A COCK

Old clay-fired rooster than can never crow,
Dark wings infolded that can never fly,
Inside, a hollow bowl that cannot flow—
We pour you full of praises from our eye.

) GREEK NECK-AMPHOR (VASE)

Lions attack a bellowing bull today
With fanged ferocity and lashing tail.
Bare-breasted, bored with all that blood, above
This dreadful scene,
Too often seen,
The sensual sirens turn away
Looking for that which women will call love,
For that desired and doomed thing, *they* call male.

) BLIND MAN

His green left hand clutches the yellow bread
With the curved, breathing motion of a sigh.
He waits, while under the unblinking head
His shoulders turn and peer like a great eye.

He does not know his jacket is dark blue.
And yet the jug his right hand has set down
(Still touching it, reluctant to let go)
Gleams with such warmth, with such a vivid hue,
He feels the color up his thin arm flow;
He hears his looking fingers whisper, Brown.

(Pablo Picasso, 1881-   )

) DON GASPAR DE GUZMAN, COUNT DUKE OF OLIVARES

This is the sort of face that sheep
Count in the night when they can't sleep.

(*Diego Rodríguez de Silva y Velázquez, 1599-1660*)

) ETRUSCAN BRONZE GREYHOUND

The girl with red nail on her thumb,
Rolling her rump and chewing gum,
The lipstick gashing her loud lips,
Pink dress too tight across her hips,
Mascara messy on her eyes,
Turns to the boy friend, "Look," she cries,
"Joey, look what the catalogue
Says is a real E-truss-can dog."

Tired from the hunt, where he brought fear
And bloody death to the light-foot deer,
In his glass cage, lean and alone,
The greyhound crunches his bronze bone.

(A dialogue)

I

Birds in blue air confide
To the painted birds inside:
Come out and be true gulls
By harbors, tides, ship hulls.
Crack the clam on the rock.
Rest on the salty dock.
Float on the wind, then dive
For floating food—alive!

II

Gulls on the canvas cry:
We do not want to fly.
Give up that garbage tide
Where many gulls have died.
Come in from the sun's brass blare
And breathe our quiet air.
Here is no wild seascape,
But absolute bare shape.
Here the defiant heart
Dies into living art.

III

The gulls flap out to sea
Screaming: our enemy
Is not the tide, but your
Death wish for that secure
Canvas which bears the taint
Of a dead painter's paint.
Why should our wing's live line
Decline into design?
Life, furious, erratic,
Alone can be ecstatic.

IV

Gulls on the painting scream:
Only the world of seem
Is permanent and pure.
Only the dead endure.
We do not lose one feather
To any wicked weather,
But one harsh thing we hate:
No mate, no mate, no mate.

V

Gulls in the salt air scream:
You dream you have a dream.
That is life twice removed.
Our flight and fall have proved
We have the feathered skill
To beat the air, but still
One thing we hate: although
We fly where blue winds blow,
And mate, and are alive,
Your painted wings survive.

VI

These answer: don't forget
Your wings are lovely, yet
You find your sweetest food
Rotting on waves, or strewed
Along the stinking mud.
The artist works with blood
And his instinctive thought.
His own quick life is caught
Like fire around a saint
And pulses in this paint.

We have no needful fight:
You are not only white
Feather flapping in light,
But the idea of flight.
I am no lifeless thing,
But a created wing.
The artist in his rage
Wept paint upon this page.
I tremble in the form
His brush made bold and warm.

The force that made you fly
Brought me without a cry
Into the painter's eye.

VII

THE
THINGS
OF
CHRISTMAS
SPEAK

) THE OX SPEAKS

When halos hovered, blinding-bright, above
Mary, Joseph, Child, I thought that mine
Would fly down to me like a blazing dove,
So that my handsome horns would wear that shine.
None came, but in a sudden greater brightness,
I saw these folk were not like those who came
To feed us in this barn. They had such whiteness
My eyes burned and I closed them in my shame.

That hot light made me thirsty. I could try
To drink out of a bucket by their stall.
But then I saw that water glowing. I
Was not fit to go near it. I went all
Troubled to muddy water near some dung.
It had a living sweetness on the tongue.

Wouldn't you be troubled if you were king
And loyal people came to you to warn
A boy they called a king had just been born?
No ruler can allow that sort of thing.
It's a matter of survival, not just hate.
I'm a family man. I didn't want to kill
Those children, only two years old, but still
I had my duty to the absolute state,

Rome, from whom my royal power runs.
I too don't like the groans through Galilee
Of mothers weeping for their murdered sons,
But my job is—find menace and remove it.
The state is children's one security,
Although I have to kill them all to prove it.

Why is it that the good word "goat" provokes
A lot of sneering laughter and cheap jokes?
A goat appears, and people start to tell
How lecherous we are, how bad we smell.
But look how stupid is that staring ox,
Those sheep that follow in their silly flocks.
We goats are quick, under these graceful horns
Our minds are graceful too, and sharp as thorns.

So when the barn was lit as if it burned
That night the child was born, I looked, and turned
And went outside alone. I would not dare
Be close to him, or touch that trembling air.
I feared that I, mere animal, plain goat,
Would breathe what he had breathed in his small throat.

The people here are proud of me. The well
I come from is a good one, deep and pure.
A stranger tasting me, eyes closed, can tell,
"Bethlehem water, drink it and be sure."
Men will come many bitter miles to slake
Their thirst with me, through all the desert perils,
The choking sand, the lion, the fanged snake,
To load my sweetness in their goatskin barrels.

I've helped men, donkeys, oxen with their thirst,
But never felt so useful as that night
The boy was born. It was that mother's first.
They washed him with me in their adoration.
I glowed then with a sudden transformation:
Light become water, water turned to light.

) THE DONKEY SPEAKS

Ox wanted his own halo. So did I.
Even the goat envied that lovely glowing.
But it was no real use for us to try.
Light wavered over us like a wind blowing,
Each of us watched it with a longing eye,
But it would not come down to bless us, knowing
We were but creatures, lucky to have the sky
To shine on straw where our own young were growing.

Yet still I had what no mere woolly sheep,
No bleating goat, no drooling ox or cow,
Could ever have: my back was strong to carry,
Tired with that winter trip, and half-asleep,
A blue cloak huddled over her bent brow,
That weary woman, that child's mother, Mary.

Feet cold, yet blistered by this rocky region,
We marched, picked soldiers of the Roman Legion,
Experts at using shield and sword and axe,
To watch these desert tribes pay up their tax.
They're poor, and they don't like it, leaving home
To pay their shekels to Imperial Rome.
One humble woman bore a boy last night.
A hard birth, but the barn was filled with light.

That child can sleep, and without any fear.
Absolute power, expressed in my bronze spear,
The skill to use it, trained into my arm,
Will keep this helpless boy from any harm.
This shaft, this blood-delighting point, I bear for
A lucky child, whom mother Rome will care for.

) THE SWADDLING CLOTHES
SPEAK

We were not elegant. Even from the start
We were just ordinary woolen cloth,
Some bits already damaged by the moth,
But we could keep the cold air from his heart.
The mother had one piece of silk and wrapped him
First in that, a pretty scrap, but found him
Chilled, so put our thick old warmth around him.
She spoke not one cross word. She never slapped him.

Since then we have been put to every use:
We have been washed in Jordan, and returned.
We've warmed a lamb, and had a goat's abuse.
One of these days we'll be thrown out and burned.
Dirty we are, but still, over the snow,
On one December night each year, we glow.

Life in the field was good. Under the sun,
Under the radiance of rain, I grew,
But worried for the future. All I knew
About the life of being straw was one
Dreadful and dreaded fact: they cut and beat you,
And threw you in a barn, on filthy mud,
Where cows would crush you as they chewed their cud,
Or, if they were too hungry, they could eat you.

But I had not been told that, when a child
Was born, clean straw was scattered underneath him,
That such a sudden light would come and wreathe him,
Even the simple straw within that wild
Fire of light would find its plain stalks turning
Into a brilliant flame, but without burning.

) THE CHILD SPEAKS

Just think of it—two fathers and one mother.
One father gave me heaven, and the other
Gave palm trees, water, donkeys with their hay,
A cross-shaped toy he made so I could play.
But mother gave three worlds—place-before-birth,
Where I was warm and safe; place-on-earth,
Where I could beg for milk and breathe live air;
Place-of-the-Spirit, which was everywhere.

I know the Wise Men and the stars have said
Some wonderful excitement lies ahead,
But right now I would rather be a child,
Happy upon the floor my father piled
With boards and nails and hammers I could walk to,
With dogs and other children I could talk to.

About the Author

PAUL ENGLE, well-known poet and novelist, was a Rhodes Scholar at Oxford and also studied at Columbia University. Though his works have usually identified him with American themes, past and present, the current collection of poems reflects his recent travels to other parts of the globe. Since 1937 he has been a member of the faculty of the University of Iowa, where he directs a world-famous creative writing program. For a number of years he edited the annual volumes of O. Henry Prize Stories. Since then he has prepared an anthology of prose and poetry by former Iowa students, entitled *Midland*.